Diesels in the Midlands

Derek Huntriss

First published 2004

ISBN 0 7110 3017 0

© Derek Huntriss 2004

Published by Ian Allan Publishing

an imprint of Ian Allan Publishing Ltd, Hersham, Surrey KT12 4RG; and printed by Ian Allan Printing Ltd., Hersham, Surrey KT12 4RG

Code: 0405/B2

Front cover: Brush/Sulzer Type 4 No D1745 arrives at Knowle & Dorridge station with the 11.45am Birkenhead Woodside to Paddington on Sunday 20 September 1964. *M. Mensing*

Rear cover: This 1956 picture shows first generation 'Derby Lightweight' 2-Car DMU Nos M79646/M79125 being shunted into platform 5 at Birmingham New Street to form the 12.20pm service to Stafford. *T. J. Edgington*

This Page: English-Electric 2,000hp 1Co-Co1 No D308 passes along the Trent Valley line west of Brinklow with the 4.40pm Euston to Stafford stopping train on Sunday 6 August 1961. *M. Mensing*

Introduction

Following nationalisation in 1948 the railways of the Midlands, almost without exception, came under the control of the Midland and Western regions of British Railways, both regions having differing policies on how the modernisation of their respective areas should be accomplished.

With its pioneering work in the development of diesel-electric shunting locomotives, the LMSR was the first company to introduce a main line diesel locomotive to work express passenger services. This locomotive was completed at Derby in 1947 and numbered 10000 and had a 16SVT 16-cylinder vee diesel engine rated at 1,600bhp. Designed primarily for use on the West Coast main line, it had a maximum speed of 93mph for a weight of 127 tons. A sister locomotive, No 10001, was completed the following year and after appropriate trials the pair were diagrammed together for the down 'Royal Scot' in 1949. With loads up to 16 coaches and over tracks not ideally suited to high-speed exploits, it was on the climbs to Shap and Beattock that the diesel locomotives showed their advantages.

The Western Region, seemingly at odds with the other regions of BR, decided in the early 1950s to adopt diesel-hydraulic locomotives; the region's top management felt that they offered certain advantages when compared with diesel-electrics. The Western Region's engineers saw the much lighter weight of the diesel-hydraulic as its main advantage and envisaged that less power would be consumed in moving its own weight, in addition to having lower building costs. In some areas of development the concept of fixed formation trains like the 'Blue Pullman', which was once considered as inflexible for operating purposes, returned as the success story of the HST.

Following the appointment of Stanley Raymond as General Manager from outside the Western, by 1962 the Region had been told to fall into line and the formulation of the National Traction Plan in 1967 envisaged the elimination of hydraulics in an effort to rationalise BR's numerous locomotive classes.

Many of the pilot scheme locomotives were often stabled in depots alongside steam locomotives and were driven with steam locomotive attitudes. They also suffered from poor maintenance facilities and the CM&EE departments often adopted the attitude that they knew better than the manufacturers with regard to such items as lubricating oils and coolants.

One of the problems with the introduction of diesel locomotives on BR was poor driver training, some drivers not being trained on the train-heating boiler, and the steam firemen were not trained on the rest of the locomotive.

The Midlands area contains a vast and complex spread of British Railways operations and in these pages a snapshot of these activities at the period of transition from steam to diesel traction is presented. In addition to the coverage of well-photographed routes there are images of long-closed cross-country routes including the Cheltenham to Stratford-upon-Avon line and the line from Peterborough to Rugby. Other closed routes featured are the former Great Central main line and the Seaton branch.

Bibliography

Adrian N. Curtis: *Western Dawn;* A&C Services
Adrian N. Curtis: *Cast of Thousands;* A&C Services
Adrian N. Curtis: *Western Liveries;* A&C Services
A. K. Butlin: *Diesel Disposal;* Coorlea Publishing
Ken Hoole: *Trains in Trouble - Vol. 3;* Atlantic Transport Publishers
Robert Stephens: *Diesel Pioneers;* Atlantic Transport Publishers
 British Rail-Main Line Gradient Profiles; Ian Allan

Magazines: *Backtrack; Modern Railways; Railway Magazine; Railway World; Traction; Trains Illustrated.*

Acknowledgements

Most railway photographers reserved their film for steam survivors and colour photographs of early diesels are scarce. I am deeply indebted to all the photographers whose work appears in these pages, and in particular to Mike Mensing, without whose contribution this title would not have been possible.

Derek Huntriss
Coventry
March 2004

Jointly designed by Metropolitan-Cammell and BR, the five 'Blue Pullman' train sets were introduced in 1959. Bringing luxurious and air-conditioned standards of comfort to the British rail traveller, seats on these luxury trains commanded supplementary fares. There were two different decorative schemes in the first class saloons: one had grey walls, blue and navy striped upholstery, a red/black carpet and polished ebony partitions, while the other had grey walls, red and navy striped upholstery, a blue and black carpet and polished rose wood partitions. The Western Pullman approaches Acocks Green with the 1pm Birmingham Snow Hill to Paddington on 12 October 1961. *M. Mensing*

Diverted via the Cheltenham to Stratford-on-Avon route because of permanent way works near Eckington on the Midland line, BR/Sulzer production 'Peak' No D30 has just passed the closed station at Cheltenham Racecourse with the 7.32am Derby to Bristol Temple Meads on Sunday 1 May 1966. The local passenger service between Cheltenham Spa St James' and Honeybourne had been withdrawn by the Western Region from 7 March 1960, but as there was no Sunday service the last trains ran on Saturday 5 March. Halts at Gretton, Hayles Abbey, Laverton, Willersey and Weston-sub-Edge were closed completely, but Winchcombe, Toddington and Broadway stations, and Bishop's Cleeve halt, remained open for parcels traffic. The official date for closure of this line was set for 3 October 1977, though no traffic had passed over it since August 1976. *M. Mensing*

Also diverted from the Midland line onto the Cheltenham to Honeybourne route, BR/Sulzer production series 'Peak' No D74 is seen 1 mile south of the closed Laverton Halt with the 9.10am Bristol Temple Meads to Newcastle on Sunday 15 May 1966. Today the section of line from Toddington to Cheltenham Racecourse is operated by the Gloucestershire Warwickshire Railway. *M.Mensing*

Below: A wintry scene on 27 December 1968 as Brush/Sulzer Type 4 No D1928 passes the site of Chipping Campden station with a Paddington train. Steam-hauled passenger workings on this route were taken over completely by diesel traction on 9 September 1964, although failures caused frequent returns to steam operation. *B. Hicks*

Right: Much of the Oxford–Worcester main line between Moreton-in-Marsh and Norton Junction, Worcester, was converted from double track to single track in early 1971. Here, Class 47 No 47077 *North Star* is seen leaving Chipping Campden Tunnel with an up working on 14 June 1975. *Neville Simms*

On 13 March 1965 Beyer-Peacock 'Hymek' B-B No D7005 climbs Honeybourne Bank with 1A22, the 11.10am Worcester–Paddington. Five months earlier, in November 1964, when the effects of the temporary withdrawals of 'Western' class diesels were at their peak, locomotive rosters between Paddington and Worcester — one of the sections worst hit by transfers away of substitute diesels — were completely reorganised, and no diesels penetrated the line for about three weeks. By the end of December matters had improved on these services and more than half of the workings had returned to 'Hymek' haulage, although Stanier Class 5 4-6-0 No 44944 found itself on the 12.05pm Hereford–Paddington on 27 December. *Bryan Hicks*

In this panoramic view of Worcester taken on Sunday 1 May 1966, BR/Sulzer 'Peak' No D30 passes Tunnel Junction signalbox as it approaches Shrub Hill station with the 7.32am Derby–Bristol Temple Meads. In addition to the extensive yards seen here, an additional freight concentration facility was opened at Sherriff Street in April 1967, handling over 1,000 tons of merchandise each week. *M. Mensing*

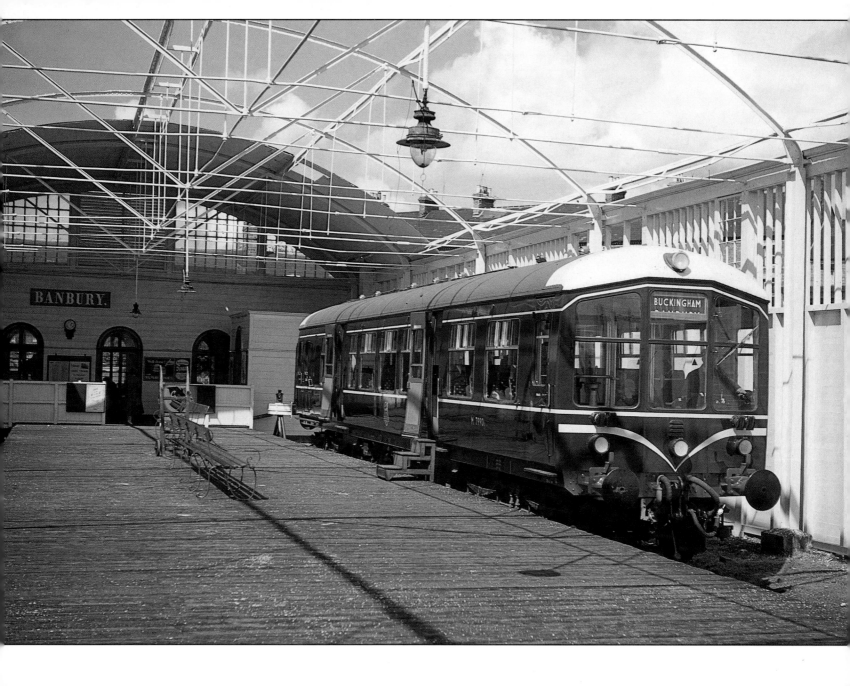

Left: 'Derby Lightweight' single-car unit No M79901 awaits departure from Banbury (Merton Street) as the 1.30pm to Buckingham on 24 August 1956. These units were seen by passengers as a vast improvement on the grubby steam-hauled stock they replaced, passenger traffic quadrupling soon after they were introduced. At the rear of the unit is the brake van end of the car which carried the exhaust pipes and had no passenger forward visibility. *T. J Edgington*

Above: English-Electric Co-Co Type 3 No D6754 is depicted at Banbury MPD on 1 December 1962 as it waits to take over a Bournemouth to York train from 'Hall' class 4-6-0 No 6906 *Chicheley Hall* and head northward over former Great Central metals. This service had been dieselised by the ER north of Banbury three months earlier, first using Darnall-based Type 3s and later with Brush Type 4s,

Left: Approaching the twilight years of its operation on BR, Class 45 No 45116 is depicted shortly after leaving Harbury Tunnel, near Leamington Spa, with the 13.07 Paddington to Birmingham and Liverpool on 22 July 1983. No 45116 was to soldier on for a further three years, its final working being the 17.03 Holyhead to York on 29 November 1986. The reason for withdrawal was a camshaft failure, its final resting place being Vic Berry's yard in Leicester, where it was scrapped in September 1988. *John Whiteley*

Right: Class 31s Nos 31260 and 31265 double-head an up express through Harbury Cutting on 27 October 1975. The production batches of Brush Type 2s were basically similar to the pilot scheme design, although the introduction of a four-panel route indicator altered their front end appearance. *Bryan Hicks*

Left: Attached to a non-corridor brake third as trailer, GWR diesel railcar No W22W is seen at Leamington Spa with a local service from Stratford-upon-Avon on 25 April 1955. The Great Western Railway introduced the railcar in the 1930s at a time when many branch lines were being closed as a result of road competition and the diesel cars seemed to be an answer. It can be said that the GWR railcars were wholly successful — in fact in 1946 the LNER borrowed Nos 6 and 19 for trials in the York area. *T. J. Edgington*

Above: A meeting of 'Westerns' at Leamington Spa on 25 July 1975. No D1011 *Western Thunderer* awaits departure for Birmingham as No D1049 *Western Monarch* brings an up working into the station. At that time both locomotives were nearing the end of their careers on BR. Unlike most 'Westerns' the withdrawal of No D1011 was planned — it was one of seven locomotives to be taken out of traffic at the end of the summer 1975 timetable. No D1049 was not to last much longer — its withdrawal coming at Laira on 26 April 1976. *Bryan Hicks*

Above: A bitterly cold 20 December 1963 sees a pair of unidentified BRCW 1,550hp Bo-Bo Type 3s climbing Hatton Bank with a Fawley–Bromford Bridge oil train. Two weeks earlier, on 2 December, the largest single trainload of petroleum products ever to run on BR was loaded at Fawley near Southampton. Made up of 54 of the largest type of high-speed rail tanks the train was over 500 yards long and had a gross weight of more than 2,000 tons. *Bryan Hicks*

Right: By contrast to the previous picture, this view of Hatton Bank taken on 10 May 1964 in beautiful spring lighting, sees Brush/Sulzer Type 4 No D1689 at the head of 1M11, the 11.10am Paddington–Birkenhead Woodside, as it nears the summit. Crew training on this route with the class had begun in November 1963, the Type 4s replacing the 'Western' class diesels which the London Midland Region did not favour. *M. Mensing*

Left: Spectators on Hatton Bank awaiting the passing of BR Class 9F 2-10-0 No 92220 *Evening Star* with a special train to Stratford-upon-Avon witness the passing of an unidentified Class 50 with an up working on 13 September 1981. The 50 members of this class were introduced by the LMR as a stop-gap before full electrification of the West Coast main line was completed between Weaver Junction and Glasgow. Once electrification was energised the class was transferred to the Western Region, a move which began in late 1972. *J. S. Whiteley*

Above: An inter-regional day excursion from Mexborough to Stratford-upon-Avon is seen as it rounds the curve to Hatton West Junction on 6 November 1965. With every generation of railway locomotives, there is always one design, which, because of its ability to perform well over a wide range of duties, is subsequently constructed in large numbers. In the diesel-electric generation this title must go to the Brush/Sulzer Type 4, seen here which in all of its variations totalled 512 locomotives. *Bryan Hicks*

A Western Region three-car suburban DMU (later Class 116) is depicted leaving the somewhat run-down station at Claverdon with the 7.36am from Stratford-upon-Avon to Leamington Spa General on 15 May 1964. This station at Claverdon was built to the west of the original one which was closed on 2 July 1939 and converted into a goods lockup, while at Bearley the platforms were lengthened and offices rebuilt. Both stations were closed to freight traffic on 20 May 1963, and Bearley, which had been partially destaffed since 17 September 1956, became an unstaffed halt from 21 June 1965. *M. Mensing*

This carefully framed picture shows Brush/Sulzer Type 4 No D1683 passing over the water troughs at Lapworth as it heads a down fitted freight over the former Great Western main line between Leamington Spa and Birmingham on 31 May 1966. No D1683 was one of the seven locomotives which were used for crew training over this route in November 1964. *M. Mensing*

Left: Another view taken on the former GWR main line at Lapworth troughs, this time depicting BR/Sulzer Bo-Bo No D7508 as it heads a down part-fitted freight on 28 June 1965. This class, later designated Class 25 under TOPS, gave sterling service in traffic, the final members being withdrawn in 1987. *M. Mensing*

Above: This view taken at Bentley Heath crossing near Knowle & Dorridge depicts an empty tank train returning from Bromford Bridge to Fawley behind BRCW Bo-Bos Nos D6544 and D6534 on 17 June 1965. Operations commenced on 3 December 1963 with five return trips per week hauled throughout by a pair of SR Type 3 diesels. *M. Mensing*

23

Seen in plain un-lined green livery, the first suburban DMUs were Derby-designed, three-car sets for the Western Region. Later to become Class 116, this one is seen waiting for departure to Great Malvern at Birmingham Snow Hill in 1958. Derby also produced large numbers of four-car sets for the Marylebone and St Pancras services, thus introducing the DMU to central London. Across the Western Region a basic standard DMU design was developed, based on the original Derby suburban sets and was built by both BRCW and the Pressed Steel Company. A similar style was used on some single-car units, these being delivered by Pressed Steel and Gloucester RCW. The introduction of these units eventually put an end to the familiar GWR auto-trains of the steam era. *T. J. Edgington*

A classic portrait of English Electric Co Bo-Bo Type 1 No D8138 as it enters Birmingham Snow Hill with a wagon and van on 11 October 1966. Not all EE Type 1s were built to the same design, D8000-D8127 being fitted with disc train reporting equipment whilst D8128-D8327 were fitted with four-character route indicators. As BR Class 20s they had a service availability of almost 90 per cent. *M. Mensing*

Left: Brush/Sulzer Type 4 No D1951 is seen approaching The Hawthorns halt with the southbound 'Pines Express' along the former GW main line between Wolverhampton and Birmingham on 15 October 1966. *M. Mensing*

Above: Also seen on the former GW main line between Birmingham and Wolverhampton is the Western Pullman DEMU on 24 April 1966. This empty stock working to Wolverhampton after servicing is approaching Hill Top tunnel west of West Bromwich. *M. Mensing*

27

One of the many first-generation DMUs introduced by BR was the series constructed by the Birmingham Railway Carriage & Wagon Co and introduced in 1957. This particularly useful type (later to become Class 104) was developed for branch line and general local services. Having shorter than normal length underfames, this class of units operated in two-, three- and four-car formations. The front windows were pitched particularly high and the cream striping had to be raised at the front corners. In this picture one of the two-car formations is moving into Dudley station to form the 4.18pm working to Walsall. It is believed that it had arrived from Dudley Port as a parcels working.
M. Mensing

English Electric Type 4 No D326 is depicted approaching Bushbury Junction, Wolverhampton, with the 8.35am Liverpool Lime Street to Birmingham New Street on Whit Sunday, 17 May 1964. Without doubt, the single most publicised event which affected any BR diesel locomotive happened to No D326 on 8 August 1963. It was hauling the 6.50pm Glasgow–Euston mail train when it was halted by signals at Sears Crossing, north of Cheddington. A masked gang had tampered with the colour light signals and then proceeded to rob the train of an estimated £2,500,000 in registered mail, bank notes and jewellery. However, this was not the only event to befall this locomotive. On 4 August 1965 it was stabled in a siding near Winson Green with no crew on board when it careered off in the direction of Birmingham New Street. At Monument Lane it crashed into a permanent way train and was derailed before being towed away to Crewe on 17 August for major repairs. *M. Mensing*

The 1 in 37 incline of the Lickey Bank is clearly visible in this view taken on 5 April 1964 as 'Peak' No D35 passes the Midland Railway signalbox on Bromsgrove station. One year later, in 1965, the common-user concept was introduced for locomotive control and maintenance on the Midland lines of the London Midland Region. The aims of this policy were threefold: to improve utilisation of diesel locomotives; to improve availability; and to make the most efficient use of staff and equipment at depots, and of fuelling and inspection points. This new system introduced the common-user concept for all diesel train locomotives. *K. Fairey*

BR/Sulzer 'Peak' No D157 is seen descending the Lickey Bank with the 7.32am Derby to Bristol Temple Meads on Sunday 23 August 1964. By late 1967 six 'Hymek' Type 3s were allocated to Worcester, of which three were stationed at Bromsgrove at any one time for banking duties on the Lickey Incline. The remainder were used on local workings around Worcester. *M. Mensing*

Below: On this day, 18 August 1962, when all banking duties on the Lickey Incline were in the hands of diesel locomotives, No D41 powers the 12-coach up 'Devonian' towards the summit near Vigo unassisted. Trials undertaken on 20 September 1961 with sister locomotive No D40 and 12-coaches were made from a standing start south of Bromsgrove station and were completed with resounding success. *Neville Simms*

Right: With the signalbox at Blackwell visible in the distance BR/Sulzer 'Peak' No D56 *The Bedfordshire and Hertfordshire Regiment* begins the descent of the Lickey Incline with the 5.55pm Birmingham New Street to Bristol Temple Meads on Sunday 9 August 1964. Becoming Class 45 No 45137 under TOPS, No D56 saw another 20 years service on BR before withdrawal in 1987. *M. Mensing*

Although not part of the initial dieselisation programme, the need for a locomotive with a rated output of between 1,500 and 2,000bhp was quickly appreciated and led to the British Railways Board placing an order for 42 units rated at 1,750bhp with the English Electric Company. Use was made of a Co bogie which was also put under the Class 55 'Deltics' and in a slightly modified form under the Class 50s. Early deliveries of what under the BRB's original classification were Type 3s went to East Anglia for use on passenger and freight work, followed by later batches to Sheffield Darnall and the then North Eastern Region. Here, one of Darnall's allocation, No D6742, is depicted $\frac{1}{2}$ mile south of Lutterworth on the Leicester to Rugby section of the former Great Central route with the 10.00am York to Bournemouth (West) on 5 March 1966. *M. Mensing*

With only two weeks to go before closure of this section of the former Great Central route Brush/Sulzer Type 4 No D1871 heads a Newcastle–Poole train away from Catesby tunnel on 20 August 1966. The longest, and most recent railway tunnel to be constructed in Northamptonshire, Catesby, was driven beneath Arbury Hill which rises to 700ft above sea level. Towards the close of the 19th century much experience had been gained in tunnelling, and mechanical appliances, unknown in Stephenson's time, were available; nevertheless Catesby was a big undertaking, commenced in February 1895 but not completed until late May 1897. Cut through lower and middle lias, very little water was encountered, and no major difficulty arose. It was 3,000yd in length, perfectly straight, but on a gradient of 1 in 176 throughout, falling towards Rugby. *Neville Simms*

Above: One of four diesel-hauled specials carrying Manchester United supporters over the former Great Central route to Wembley for the FA Cup final against Leicester on 25 May 1963 is hauled by one of Sheffield Darnall's allocation of English Electric Type 3s, No D6802, which is seen passing the station at Rugby Central. *Neville Simms*

Right: Brush/Sulzer Type 4 No D1773 is depicted arriving at Nottingham Victoria with a Newcastle–Poole train on 31 August 1966. Main line passenger trains ceased working through Nottingham Victoria on 3 September 1966, leaving only the local services to Grantham and Rugby which were worked by DMUs. *Peter Fitton*

A classic view of English Electric Type 4 No D322 as it heads the up 'Caledonian' alongside the recently constructed M1 motorway near Welton, south of Rugby, on 6 June 1962. No D322 was the first member of the class to be withdrawn, in 1967, following a severe accident one year earlier on 14 May 1966. Both of the locomotive crew were killed in the crumpled front-end when several hopper wagons loaded with soda-ash broke away from a preceding train on the incline at Moore, south of Warrington. No D322 was hauling the 20.40 Euston to Stranraer boat train. Rugby and Edge Hill cranes assisted in clearing the wreckage and No D322 was removed to Crewe. *Peter Fitton*

Seen approaching Rugby on the spur line near Clifton Mill on 22 May 1965, Brush/Mirrlees Type 2 No D5551 is in charge of the 12.40pm Harwich (Town) to Rugby (Midland) via Peterborough and Market Harborough. A few weeks earlier, on 10 March, BR/Sulzer Type 2 No D5011 had caught fire on this route at Yelvertoft & Stanford Park whilst hauling a Market Harborough to Rugby local. *M. Mensing*

Left: Pilot scheme Type 4 'Peak' No D4 *Great Gable* has its train heating boiler replenished at Rugby (Midland) station whilst working the 8.20am Carlisle to London (Euston) on 23 December 1961. This exercise was not normally necessary as the locomotive would have taken water from the troughs at Newbold which on this day were frozen over. The 10 2,300hp pilot scheme locomotives were designated Class ML4; they were initially allocated to Crewe for use on fast passenger and parcels duties between Euston and Glasgow. The engines for these 10 locomotives were supplied from Sulzer's Winterthur works in Switzerland.

Right: Another view of a pilot scheme locomotive taken at Rugby (Midland), this time being the prototype BR/Sulzer Type B No D5000. Here the locomotive awaits departure with the 12.35pm for London (Euston) via Northampton.
Both: Neville Simms

Left: The overhead catenaries have yet to appear in this view showing simultaneous departures of English Electric Type 4s as they head for the north from Rugby (Midland) on 9 September 1963. No D351 is at the head of a Liverpool express alongside No D231 which is working a down parcels train. Electrification was extended southward from Nuneaton to Rugby on 4 January 1965. *Bryan Hicks*

Above: Another English Electric Type 4 heading north from Rugby. This time No D381 is working the 10.40am from London (Euston) to Blackpool and Holyhead on 7 April 1962. The Western Lines electrification programme was further extended on 3 January 1966 when the Rugby to Coventry section of the Birmingham main line was energised. *Peter Fitton*

Split-headcode English-Electric Type 4 No D344 heads an up Llandudno express west of Brinklow, between Rugby and Nuneaton, on 16 March 1963. This train, which arrived at Rugby at 1.25pm, was more often hauled by steam motive power, the photographer, a dedicated steam enthusiast, being somewhat disappointed. This locomotive, which became 40144 under the TOPS renumbering system, was to survive in traffic until May 1981 and after after one month in store at Reddish was finally broken up at BREL's Swindon Works in September 1983. *Neville Simms*

The Oxford Canal at Nettle Hill near Shilton, between Rugby and Nuneaton, has a coating of ice in this late afternoon view of English Electric Type 4 No D382 heading a London (Euston) to Blackpool train on Christmas Eve, 24 December 1962. The LMR had received its first batch of the class by the late spring of 1959, allocations going to Camden, Crewe and Carlisle Upperby. *Neville Simms*

Electrification is well in evidence in this picture taken at Nuneaton on 31 May 1963 as the prototype English Electric 2,700hp Co-Co No DP2 passes through with a down Blackpool working. When introduced onto West Coast main line duties on the London Midland Region in May 1962 No DP2's diagram embraced the 7.45am Euston to Liverpool and 2.0pm back, then the 7.15am Euston–Perth as far as Crewe and, it was believed, the 'West Coast Postal' back. After a mishap at Camden depot it was returned to the Vulcan Foundry on 22 May. At the time this picture was taken No DP2 was covering one of the 'Deltic' prototype's former diagrams, working the Perth portion of the 1.25pm Euston–Blackpool and Perth through to Carlisle and returning to London each night with the 9.0pm from Perth. *Neville Simms*

Another picture taken at Nuneaton (Trent Valley) on 31 May 1963 sees one of the LMS/English Electric Co 1,600bhp Co-Co prototypes, No 10001, as it works a Fleetwood (Wyre Dock) to Broad Street fish train. The ex-LMS diesel twins, Nos 10000 and 10001, had been barred from single-unit passenger workings in 1961 because of inadequate train heating boiler performance. *Neville Simms*

Below: Diverted over the Nuneaton to Coventry line on Sunday 4 September 1966 English Electric 2,000hp 1Co-Co1 diesel-electric No D219 *Caronia* passes through the station at Chilvers Coton with the 4.15pm Birmingham (New Street) to Euston. This train had been diverted due to electrification work taking place between Birmingham New Street and Coventry. *M. Mensing*

Right: Totally immaculate English-Electric Type 4 No D308 stands in the rebuilt station at Coventry with the stock of the Royal Train on 4 July 1963. On this occasion the Royal Train had conveyed the Queen on her visit to the Royal Agricultural Show at Kenilworth. On the other end of the train was another equally immaculate English Electric Type 4, No D371. *Raymond Reed*

Above: Much to the disappointment of the photographer who was expecting one of Liverpool (Edge Hill's) 'Princess Royal' class Pacifics, English Electric Type 4 No D218 heads the up 'Merseyside Express' near Atherstone on 9 September 1961. The locomotive is carrying the plain green livery first adopted for this class in 1958. This green was a perpetuation of the steam age 'express passenger' colour and was applied to most of the first-generation diesels. *Neville Simms*

Right: Yet to receive the addition of a yellow warning panel, English Electric Type 4 No D316 rounds Queensville Curve near Stafford with a down parcels train on 6 October 1962. On the London Midland Region the EE Type 4s fought a rearguard action along the West Coast main line to Euston in the face of advancing electrification and towards the end of their careers the class saw little all-year-round passenger work. *M. Mensing*

EE Type 4 No D326 attracts attention from onlookers as it passes through the old station at Stafford with the up 'Royal Scot' on 4 March 1961. The reconstructed passenger station at Stafford was officially opened on 31 December 1962, a week before inauguration of electric traction between Crewe and Stafford. The new station, which was built on the old site, entailed demolition of the existing buildings and extensive temporary buildings were necessary during reconstruction. Associated track remodelling provided down and up slow (to the west) and down and up fast tracks continuously from east of Milford & Brocton (near the exit of Shugborough tunnel) to Crewe, and transferred one flat intersection of tracks (involving down fast and up slow) from Stafford to the latter point, so relieving Stafford of this crossing. *M. Mensing*

It was in 1952 when the British Transport Commission decided that the answer to the particular problem of local and branch line services would be the introduction of diesel multiple-units. They were instantly popular with passengers who thought that they were a decided improvement on the dirty and antiquated steam-hauled stock they replaced. The Birmingham Railway Carriage & Wagon Co's first-generation DMUs were introduced in 1957 and were of low-density configuration, having shorter than the normal 57ft underframes. They were operated in two-, three-, and four-car formations. These features are well seen in this view of a three-car formation passing Pinfold Crossing as it leaves Uttoxeter on 19 August 1961 with the 7.3pm service to Stoke-on-Trent. Unlike other units in this class, the one illustrated is not carrying the very decorative 'speed whiskers'.
M. Mensing

Left: This interesting picture shows Brush/Sulzer Type 4 No 47478, which still carries the silver roof it received at Stratford depot, as it passes Hednesford with a diverted morning Liverpool to Southampton train on 9 April 1989. This train, which had left the West Coast main line at Rugeley, was routed to proceed to Birmingham via Walsall. *Gavin Morrison*

Above: A much earlier picture, taken at Birmingham New Street on 16 June 1962, depicts BR/Sulzer Production Series 'Peak' (later Class 46 No 46011) No D148 as it arrives at platform 9 with the 12.52pm York to Bristol Temple Meads. The first locomotive of this batch, No D138, had appeared on BR at the end of 1961, the remainder having been delivered by February 1963. *M. Mensing*

Above: Timetabled to run via Nuneaton due to electrification works between Birmingham and Coventry, this train, hauled by English Electric Type 4 No D230 *Scythia*, is approaching Whitacre station with the 10.8am from New Street to Euston on Sunday 3 May 1962. The line from Whitacre to Midland Junction (Nuneaton) celebrated its centenary two years later on 1 November 1964.

Right: Another Sunday diversion, this time due to electrification work on the Trent Valley Line, sees the up 'Ulster Express' leaving Beechwood tunnel, between Birmingham (New Street) and Coventry on 25 June 1961. This train is being hauled by English-Electric Type 4 No D302, still wearing its original plain green livery with red buffer beams and without a yellow warning panel. *Both: M. Mensing*

Left: Originally the experimental golden ochre-liveried Brush Type 2 No D5579, Class 31 No 31161 heads a goods train towards Coalville past Moira West Junction on 7 May 1987.

Below: Green-liveried BR/Sulzer Class 25 No 25038 pilots sister locomotive No 25272 as they head a train of 24-ton VB hoppers into Derby on 29 May 1974. *Both: Hugh Ballantyne*

Above: A spectacular view of Derby Locomotive Works taken from the top of the coaling stage on 16 August 1966. In addition to ex-works locomotives, No 10000, the LMS prototype main-line diesel locomotive, lies between two of the SR-designed prototypes, all withdrawn from traffic in December 1963. A product of a close liaison between the LMS, under CME H. G. Ivatt, and English Electric, No 10000 had appeared in late 1947, followed by No 10001 after nationalisation.

Right: Another view from the same vantage point sees four newly-constructed BR/Sulzer Bo-Bos, Nos D7619-D7622. Eventually a total of 477 of these locomotives were built, D7667 holding the honour of being the 1,000th diesel locomotive to be constructed at Derby. The first 151 members of this class were later designated BR Class 24, the remainder, having an uprated 1,250hp Sulzer engine and re-designed body, becoming Class 25. *Both: Ken Fairey*

Left: A general view of the diesel depot at Shirebrook taken on 7 September 1977 shows Class 47 and Class 56 locomotives. The depot was once somewhat incorrectly described in a magazine caption as adjacent to the station but Shirebrook once boasted three stations. The adjacent station referred to was the remnants of the MR station. Other stations were Langwith Junction and Shirebrook South. To avoid confusion the ex-MR station was latterly officially Shirebrook West.

Above: Another depot view, this time showing the former steam shed at Westhouses on a very gloomy 27 March 1967. Maintenance of the early diesel locomotives presented a major problem, many engines having to share outdated and unsuitable facilities with steam. This problem was eventually addressed by the construction of purpose-built diesel depots, the first of these being the former steam depot at Devons Road in north London. *Both: Ken Fairey*

Above: This view taken on 14 April 1981 shows BR corporate blue-liveried Class 47 No 47329 heading a train of empty coal wagons past the vast marshalling yards at Toton. The 'Corporate Identity' programme heralded new liveries and 'house' styles for the whole railway system and was introduced in early 1965. Also launched at this time was the distinctive 'double arrow' symbol. Applied without any lining, the blue had a particular starkness. *J. S. Whiteley*

Right: Also seen in the unlined BR corporate blue livery are Class 20s Nos 20157 and 20121 as they leave Nottingham with the 12.05 Skegness–Leicester on 17 August 1985. The first of these highly successful machines was formally handed over by the English Electric company to the British Transport Commission on 3 June 1957. Primarily intended for freight services, they could be used at speeds up to 75mph on passenger trains. *Hugh Ballantyne*

Left: This 29 May 1978 view sees Class 47 No 47514 arriving at the south end of Loughborough Midland station with an up express. Clearly seen in the picture are the delicate glass and iron platform canopies, the apexes of which formerly supported slender finials, some of which have unfortunately disappeared.

Below: Another view at Loughborough Midland taken on 29 May 1978 shows the station from the north end. Here Class 45 No 45111 *Grenadier Guardsman* is seen departing with the 12.08 St Pancras–Nottingham train. The world famous Brush Locomotive works is clearly visible behind the locomotive. *Both: Gavin Morrison*

Left: Class 31 No 31231 comes off the Nuneaton Goods Curve at Wigston South Junction with a signalling engineer's train on 19 April 1985. The Midland route was one of the last main lines to retain mechanical signalling, multiple aspect colour lights not arriving until 1987. The Midland Railway saw its 150th anniversary in 1994. The railway left its mark on the infrastructure and many examples have achieved 'listed structures' status and remain in use to this day. *Hugh Ballantyne*

Above: Here a much earlier view, taken on 4 June 1966, shows BR/Sulzer Type 2 No D5145 (later Class 24) approaching Market Harborough near the Midland main line crossing with the 12.40pm Harwich to Rugby Midland on what was the last day of services over this route. After this date the Rugby to Peterborough East and Seaton to Luffenham lines ceased to function. After closure notices were posted in January 1966, all except emergency maintenance was suspended and, as in this view, the track was akin to looking across a field. *M. Mensing*

In this view a two-car Gloucester Railway Carriage & Wagon Co DMU is seen leaving Seaton with the 8.15am to Stamford on 28 May 1966. Seaton station, situated on the slopes of the Welland Valley dominated at this point by the Harringworth Viaduct of the Midland Railway's Glendon South Junction to Manton line, was perfectly suited to the enthusiast who liked his railways in a rural setting. Bursts of activity punctuated long periods of inactivity although almost all the 'main line' Peterborough to Rugby trains had their connecting branch trains to Uppingham and Stamford. During January 1965 the tracks in Seaton goods yard were removed and signalling simplified. *M. Mensing*

Heading south on the Midland main line ½ mile south of Desborough station is production series 'Peak' No D104 as it works the 11.35am Bradford Forster Square to St Pancras on 19 March 1966. Becoming Class 45 No 45063 under TOPS, this locomotive survived in traffic on BR until 6 May 1986 when it suffered a triple pump failure, after which it was broken up at Vic Berry's yard. *M. Mensing*

Left: Class 31 No 31422 and Class 25 No 25254 are seen coming off the Corby line at Glendon Junction with a coal train on 22 April 1975. The Midland main line from St Pancras is four-tracked between Kentish Town and Glendon South Junction. Between Bedford and Wellingborough the main and goods lines are on different levels to give an easier gradient for the heavier coal trains while the passenger lines climb steeply over Sharnbrook summit. The sinuous nature of the Midland main line has pronounced curves through Wellingborough and Kettering with more severe ones at Market Harborough and Wigston.

Above: On the four-track section south of Glendon Junction Class 44 No 44005 *Cross Fell* heads a down goods for the Corby line on 22 April 1975. As more diesels became available for work on the West Coast main line the original 10 'Peaks' were reallocated from Camden to Toton in April 1962 where they were to spend the rest of their days relegated to freight duties. Soon after transfer they were noted on class 'J' coal hauls to Castle Donington and on Toton to Wichnor freights. No 44005 was withdrawn from Toton in April 1978 and was broken up at Derby Works. *Both: Hugh Ballantyne*

Above: Another view taken near Glendon North Junction shows Class 45 No 45137 *The Bedfordshire and Hertfordshire Regiment (TA)* with an up St Pancras train on 22 April 1975. This locomotive appears to have suffered some front end damage but was to continue in traffic until 15 June 1987 when a cracked block forced its withdrawal. Its last revenue earning duty was hauling 1E16 from Liverpool to Newcastle on 27 May 1987.

Right: Framed by the attractive cast details of the columns and supports for Kettering's station roof, Class 45 No 45142 approaches with a down fast service from St Pancras on 9 June 1982. At this time the station site had already suffered rationalisation and an extension to the car park. A 1984 scheme to resignal the route between Wellingborough and Loughborough replaced 24 manual boxes with one box at Leicester. *Both: Hugh Ballantyne*

Left: Seen with a loaded Redland aggregates train, Class 31s Nos 31213 and 31107 are approaching Kettering Junction on the up slow line on 10 May 1983. The production series locomotives of this class were basically similar to the pilot scheme design, although the introduction of a four-panel route indicator altered their front end appearance. *H. Ballantyne*

Below: Class 45 No 45144 *Royal Signals* is depicted leaving Wellingborough on 16 April 1982 with the 10.12 Sheffield to St Pancras. No 45144 was to survive until 18 December 1987. when it became derailed whilst hauling 5C26 Bristol to Malago Vale ECS. *John Whiteley*

Below: Class 45 No 45114 is seen heading a down express through Wellingborough on 16 August 1980. The sinuous nature of this part of the Midland main line is apparent, with pronounced curves through Wellingborough and Kettering and more severe ones at Wigston and Market Harborough.

Right: Another view at Wellingborough on 16 August 1980 shows Class 45 No 45146 as it heads an up express past Finedon Road box. This was the busiest and largest box in the area, although like so many more locations, the yards here saw only a fraction of the goods traffic handled in earlier years. *Both: Gavin Morrison*

Index of Locations

Ian Allan
PUBLISHING

Full details of Ian Allan Publishing
titles can be found on
www.ianallanpublishing.com
or by writing for a free copy of
our latest catalogue to:
Marketing Dept., Ian Allan Publishing,
Riverdene Business Park,
Molesey Road, Hersham KT12 4RG.

For an unrivalled range of aviation, military,
transport and maritime publications, visit our secure
on-line bookshop at
www.ianallansuperstore.com

or visit the Ian Allan Bookshops in
Birmingham
47 Stephenson Street, B2 4DH;
Tel: 0121 643 2496;
e-mail: ia-birmingham@btconnect.com
Cardiff
31 Royal Arcade, CF10 1AE;
Tel: 02920 390615;
e-mail: ia-cardiff@btconnect.com
London
45/46 Lower Marsh, Waterloo, SE1 7RG;
Tel: 020 7401 2100;
e-mail: ia-waterloo@btconnect.com
Manchester
5 Piccadilly Station Approach, M1 2GH;
Tel: 0161 237 9840;
e-mail: ia-manchester@btconnect.com

and (aviation and military titles only) at
The Aviation Experience,
Birmingham International Airport
3rd Floor, Main Terminal, B26 3QJ;
Tel: 0121 781 0921
e-mail: ia-bia@btconnect.com

or through mail order by writing to:
Ian Allan Mail Order Dept.,
4 Watling Drive, Hinckley LE10 3EY.
Tel: 01455 254450.
Fax: 01455 233737.
e-mail: midlandbooks@compuserve.com

You are only a visit away from over 1,000
publishers worldwide.